HOW TO DRESS FOR BUSINESS

"BUILD YOUR SUIT OF ARMOUR"

BY D.F.MCKEEVER

AMAZON EDITION

ISBN:9781791944995

COPYRIGHT 2011 D.F.MCKEEVER

DISCLAIMER & PRIVACY POLICY THIS BOOK IS LICENSED FOR YOUR PERSONAL ENJOYMENT ONLY. THIS IS THE SOLE PROPERTY OF DESIGNOVATION. ALL RIGHTS ARE RESERVED. NO PART OF THIS WORK MAY BE REPRODUCED OR TRANSMITTED IN ANY FORM OR BY ANY MEANS; ELECTRONIC OR MECHANICAL, INCLUDING, PHOTOCOPYING, RECORDING OR BY ANY INFORMATION STORAGE OR RETRIEVAL SYSTEM, WITHOUT THE WRITTEN PERMISSION OF THE COPYRIGHT OWNER. DESIGNOVATION SHALL NOT BE HELD LIABLE TO ANY PERSON OR ENTITY WITH RESPECT TO ANY LOSS OR DAMAGE CAUSED OR ALLEGED TO BE CAUSED DIRECTLY OR INDIRECTLY BY THE INFORMATION CONTAINED WITHIN THIS WORK. FURTHERMORE, NO PART OF THIS MAY BE REPRINTED OR RESOLD. THIS EBOOK MAY NOT BE RE-SOLD OR GIVEN AWAY TO OTHER PEOPLE. IF YOU WOULD LIKE TO SHARE THIS BOOK WITH ANOTHER PERSON, PLEASE PURCHASE AN ADDITIONAL COPY FOR EACH RECIPIENT. IF YOU'RE READING THIS BOOK AND DID NOT PURCHASE IT, OR IT WAS NOT PURCHASED FOR YOUR USE ONLY, THEN PLEASE RETURN TO AMAZONBOOKS.COM THANK YOU FOR RESPECTING THE WORK OF THIS AUTHOR.

LEARN MORE: HTTP://WWW.DESIGNOVATION.CO.UK/ABOUT

Contents

	Page
PART ONE	
Introduction	4
Chapter 1: Visual Communication	9
Chapter 2: Brand Image	20
Chapter 3: Colour	27
Chapter 4: Uniforms & Dress codes	34
Chapter 5: Uniform Suppliers & Fittings	42
Chapter 6: Personal & Professional Image	47
PART TWO	
Chapter 7: Colours	52
Chapter 8: Uniforms & Dress codes	58
Chapter 9: Accessorise	93
Chapter 10: The Capsule wardrobe	96
Chapter 11: Personal & Professional Image	102
Chapter 12: Personal & Professional Image: Interviews	105
Chapter 13: Personal & Professional Image: Presentations	114
Chapter 14: Care & Repair, Stain removal, Care Symbols	119
Chapter 15: Conclusion	126
Summary	129
Bibliography & Reference Material	131
Customer Training Quotes	133

Introduction

Over the years I have observed how visual communication impacts on people's lives and careers. It has taken me on an interesting journey discovering the power of clothing as an essential business tool which I refer to as "your suit of armour". It is a necessary tool for every business person whether you're a company director, freelance professional, micro business or large corporation.

Through my interest in business I decided that the business world needs at least one book on this subject. It ceases to amaze me that even in this day and age most companies from your micro business to corporation don't take financial account of the impact and relevance of their "staff's" image.

I first discovered the power of clothing very early on as an unconfident youth. I loved experimenting with my creative and artistic skills through designing and making my own clothes. This is where I discovered my motivation to inspire others confidence and self esteem through clothing, having experienced first hand the confidence my clothing creations gave me motivating my choice to study fashion design. Unfortunately my enthusiasm for the Fashion Industry was short lived after graduating from Fashion design, slowly realising that the fashion industry is motivated by the ego of designers and profits in the majority of cases rather than needs and care of the consumer never mind the consumer's confidence or self esteem.

My motivation to inspire others confidence and self esteem led me to train as a Colour & Image consultant where I discovered an alternative route to empowering others with my knowledge of personal development and creativity. Coming from a family of entrepreneurs and mentored in business from a very early age I quickly found a new avenue for combining my passion for business and clothing by providing training and seminars on developing your professional image for the unemployed, carers, youth and graduate groups. This progressed to training for management and business groups which later lead to the establishing of my business of 18 years in the contract management and supply of professional business wear and uniforms.

In this book "How to Dress for Business" we highlight a subject rarely discussed and often dismissed in business your "Professional Image" a key factor to building a congruent brand image. The book is designed in two parts. Part one provides a narrative sharing my experiences over the years that demonstrate the essential elements of "Dressing for Business" and Part two provides a series of practical templates, formulas and charts for referencing and guidance.

Corporations spend millions of pounds every year on their marketing activities for brand development but often dismiss the most obvious and essential ingredient their "staff". That "first impressions" of you and your employees will either build or destroy your consumer's perception and confidence of your products, services and brand and directly affect your companies' profitability in an increasingly competitive global market.

From my experiences as a designer, image consultant and corporate wear business owner and supplier my goal is to provide the tools and knowledge on how to evaluate the correct needs for your company to create a visual representation of your companies values, ethos and culture through you and your staff's professional image.

In this book we begin by discussing communication and the importance of image as a visual communicator and the different facets of image that influence people, consumers and your customers.

Before we look in detail at image, clothing, dress codes and grooming we look at the basic foundation to any corporate image "your brand". We demonstrate that a well designed "name and logo" is essential to define first the message and values of your company. With the foundation of a good brand you can create a strong visual interface with your customer and build a congruent image that flows effortlessly through your organisation.

We discuss what type of organisations and departments within organisations should dismiss uniforms and dress codes, where personal freedom and self expression are necessary and essential to profit, growth and attracting new staff.

My business ethos is to share an ethical and sustainable approach to image rather than following the "fashion industry" business model. We promote an investment in quality timeless classics by demystifying style, image and colour. We discuss the importance and relevance of confidence, colour, styling, grooming and accessorising, introducing the powerful tools of colour analysis and the capsule wardrobe.

Finally we provide reference material and samples that you can dip into on dress code policies, dressing for interviews & presentations, storing, caring and repairing your uniforms all essential on " How to Dress for Business".

PART ONE

Chapter 1

Visual Communication

Many years ago I was invited as a young entrepreneur to attend the first Entrepreneurial Convention in the European Parliament in Brussels, one evening during a dinner for some of the British delegates I met a retired gentlemen who was a representative and volunteer for a leading British entrepreneur charity where we had an in depth conversation on the subject of image.

He recalled for me his first job as a young apprentice in the 1940's in journalism, where on arriving for his first day at work he was sent to the Editors office, on Bond Street.

I waited patiently for over an hour in the Editors reception, only to be instructed by the secretary that I was to spend the day standing on the corner of Bond Street, with one clear instruction "to people watch", and not to return until the end of the day.

At the end of the day I returned to the Editors office where the secretary told me to go home and return the next day.

The next day I returned to his office as instructed and waited patiently. Finally the editor appeared in the reception instructing his secretary that he would be back in 30 minutes, at that the Editor turned and nodded and gestured for me to follow him. As he walked briskly downstairs and out onto Bond Street he asked

"So George what did you learn yesterday? "

Nervously, I answered there's a lot of people on Bond Street.

The editor took me to the corner of Bond Street and stepping backwards into the recess of a closed door way asked "What do you see, George?"

Before you start any career in journalism the most valuable lesson I can teach you is this;
"People can tell you a million things without uttering a single word, and if you want to learn one of the most valuable communication tools in life and master journalism, you must first learn how to read people. Many stories can be told by our appearance, clothing, grooming, posture, facial expressions; it communicates

our personality, attitude, emotions, economical and social status, sophistication and success."

He maintained that no matter what generation or culture you come from, whether you are standing on Bond Street in London, Time Square in New York, standing in a room full of strangers or meeting someone for the first time before you open your mouth you have already told your story and firmly established that very important "first impression" rightly or wrongly.

Principle One; Image matters.

Principle Two; Be honest with your customer, what is your company really about?

Consumers today are exceptionally image savvy and due to the volume of subliminal marketing and advertising that we are bombarded with daily we are all acutely aware if the image being painted for us is false or incongruent with your brand and marketing message.

Many successful companies like Pixar Studios & Innocents (Health drinks) thrive because they are totally transparent and genuine about their priorities as a company. They realised from day one that there was no place for dress codes or uniforms because their organisation is primarily about self expression and creativity and serve their customers by ensuring the integrity of their creativity in every aspect of their business.

Other international companies i.e. Disney, McDonalds, Burger King, KFC, UPS etc realise that a uniform and dress code must be executed precisely and is essential to their brand identity, company success and profitability because their role is to serve the customers needs before their needs as an employee.

Clothing and image can be a very emotive issue for many people, because primarily it is a major part of self expression and personal identity. Secondly many of our clothing choices are made emotionally rather than rationally. When being honest about your company culture you have to face up to one of the biggest arguments and challenge which I have always had; addressing the balance between personal freedom of self expression which I passionately believe in and the lack of common sense where a strict disciplined image is essential in the workplace. Customers today expect and demand leadership, confidence and assertiveness from a company and brand.

First and foremost individuals must accept even in the 21st century there are clearly defined careers where their primary function and role is to serve the customer. Personal image and identity are irrelevant where a disciplined image, uniform and dress code are both essential and necessary to communicate authority, confidence, respect and maintain order & safety i.e. Police, Fire Service, Military, Immigration, Legal profession, Aviation etc.

A typical example is the case of the 70's Air stewardess's, who had been issued with overtly feminine uniforms with no authoritative value. Passenger's lives were put at risk as well meaning male passenger's put the air stewardess's off the plane after a crash landing leaving no one qualified & trained to get the remaining passengers safely off the plane.

A good professional image or uniform when executed correctly will convey authority and confidence and demand attention and respect in various roles of responsibility. Within these roles attention to details in dress code are essential the simplest bending of the rules can totally destroy the effectiveness of an otherwise very effective uniform.

I recall an occasion where I met two young Police officers. One of the officer's credibility was totally undermined due to his unshaven appearance, the visibility of a large tattoo below his short sleeved shirt and the wearing of a chunky tight silver neck chain and wrist bracelet.

The subconscious messages sent by his personal grooming, styling and accessories sent a series of very mixed messages that conflicted with his professional role. His need to express his personal style and identity overshadowed and dominated his professional role.

Like wise understanding the culture of your business is essential; if you are a traditional British, American or Western cultured business your focus will quite probably be on selling your products, brand and company to the consumer where your image will relate largely to your consumer. Compared to Japan where their business culture is about selling your company to your employees where image or uniforms are more relevant to the team and the needs of their staff.

Principle Three; Your staff's image must serve the needs of both your customer and your employee.

The *third principle* recognises that your staff's image has to serve and motivate two separate individual needs, one is the needs of your *customer* and the second is the needs of your *employee*. Your goal is to understand and meet the needs of both or in some circumstances prioritise one over the other, for example; Pixar studios primary goal is to ignite and support their employees in a creative and energetic working environment. In an organisation where employees have no or limited contact with the end consumer a uniform would be a destructive obstacle to expressing their creativity in Pixar the employee's needs are paramount.

Paradoxically with a company such as British Airways cabin crew, the customer is king their role as a company is to first and foremost demonstrate through their image; authority, confidence, professionalism and assertiveness. Their role is to execute a first class level of service and maintain a reasonable level of authority and reassurance for issuing safety or security measures in the event of an accident.

Image has a dramatic influence on our customers. Companies spend thousands of pounds every year on expensive branding campaigns, logo design, web design, marketing material, ad campaigns, vehicle signage and interiors because they understand that their customers perception and image of them matters. What is remarkable though is that they often forget about the people who execute, perform and provide those services and products to the consumer their most important selling tool their *employees.*

Many years ago I arrived at a new client's office and was blown away by the time and expense the business had invested in creating beautifully designed offices that promoted their brand and marketing message. The interior was welcoming and co-ordinated in the Companies brand colours which flowed through every component in the room from the carpets, upholstered furniture, fixtures, fittings paint work to accessories. Their brand continuity, their grasp and understanding of selling their brand and company message to the consumer was perfect. But then…………… the bomb shell………..a woman, my first personal contact with the company walked in the room……Her choice of attire for the day included a loose fitting bright vest top, hip length shorts, bare legs and open toe flat sandals.

Still to this day, I find it very hard to erase that image from my mind "*the employee is the business*" they are our ambassadors and a reflection of our capabilities, strengths and professionalism as a business. Without our people we may as well just shut up shop. The outcome of my visit resulted in the implementation of a fully branded uniform when the brand image was finally complete the biggest transformation was of the woman I met that day.

Her new uniform communicated the company message with an image that stated professionalism from the personalised uniform with corporate scarf and co-ordinating tailored clothes & court shoes, the brand image was complete.

But more importantly something else had changed ……….her confidence was transformed and self evident in the change in her posture, walk, eye contact, confidence and assertiveness.

Ultimately your image must serve the needs and expectations of both your *customer* and your *staff*. The bonus is that for both you and your staff in many cases you are providing much more than just a uniform. For those with least confidence and great potential it can become a secret tool their *"suit of armour"*. When executed correctly a personalised image, clothing, uniforms and dress codes can provide motivation and inspiration to the most unlikely of employees. The goal of "The Business Dress code" is about how everyone in your organisation can benefit from the correct professional image.

Through my research on the subject of visual communication I have came to understand that image has a great influence in 21st century business; Here are just a few quotes from professional organisations surveyed on the topic of personal image and presentation. Survey of 300 U.K. Financial and Personnel Directors; 93% Top Decision Makers agreed;

1. Personal Presentation was the key factor to gaining employment.

2. More senior the executive; more emphasise was made that image was said to be vital to job success and advancement and had direct impact on company profitability, especially through the implementing of corporate clothing.

3. Emphasis of personal presentation for; Sales, Marketing, Human Resources, Finance & Accounts.

4. Managing and Personnel Directors considered a good Image more important than holding a Post Graduate Degree.

The above statements highlight how important image is whether through a uniform, dress code policy or personal choice of clothing for work.

Summary

Principle One; Image matters.

Principle Two; Be honest with your customer, what is your company really about.

Principle Three; Your staff's image must serve the needs of both your *customer* and your *employee*.

Chapter 2

Brand Image

Before we even discuss dress codes and uniforms the foundation of any successfully business image must begin with an intelligent and well designed "company name and logo" in a word your brand.

I am amazed by the amount of companies who at the inception of their business spend hours and hundreds of pounds on business plans and cash flow projections and then make one of the most costly mistakes they will ever make by not seeking professional advice on their company name and brand.

It is essential that you employ professional expertise on the design of your brand to ensure it reflects the correct message for your company, your industry and your consumer.

Principle Four; the visual representation of your business starts with your company brand, it is the template for every other visual element of your business.

You often hear stories from customers who spent an hour over a cup of coffee coming up with a business name and then ask their young nephew or niece who is fabulous at Art to put together their company logo. Only to find out a year down the line they realise they got the name and brand all wrong, someone else has the trademark on it, they don't have the essential URL's and have to re brand. By which time they have lost thousands of pounds on lost marketing, customer loyalty and brand recognition on a name and brand that doesn't work.

With a well executed brand you can visually distinguish your self in the market place and leverage the power of your image. The same principles of communication and design apply to branding and uniform image it is essential to understand the significance of; visual communication, colour, styling and symbolism.

"1st Impressions are created within the 1st 30 second, a first impression is based on; 55% how you look, 38% how you sound, 7% what you actually say."

In 2012 our lives are dictated and influenced consciously and subconsciously by branding. Our corporate culture and society has become so sensitive to the subtleties and importance of image that every business no matter how big or small must take serious consideration to their brand identity and image. To succeed in a global economy your brand image must be congruent and seamless from your management and staff image, premises and interiors, to your vehicles and signage, web design to stationary & marketing literature. Your visual communication with the customer is paramount due to the pace and choice of mediums now used by consumers when making decisions and choices to buy.

Principle Five: *The essential ingredients to a successful brand are; name, visibility, colour, styling.*

A professional and commercial design company should have an essential grasp of business and design. You need a design team that can help with the creative thinking process to help select the most marketable business name and put your business interests before creativity when it comes to your logo & brand design.

Name

Your name must first be available; does anyone else own the company name? Is the name available as a domain .com, limited company, trademark name and symbol? The last thing you want is a letter from an

Intellectual Property Lawyer telling you that you are infringing on another companies brand or trademark.

What does your name translate, convey, imply? Is it communicating action, emotion, humour or intellect?

Is it short, clear, memorable, unique, distinguishable, simple and instantly recognisable?

One of the most costly lessons I ever made in branding was choosing to misspell my business name. During my 17 years supplying uniforms the misspelling of my company name caused a variety of problems for customers; confused identity with other companies, wrongly written cheques, customer frustration trying to find our web site trying to remember the correct misspelling.

Visibility

Visibility is one aspect of brand design often overlooked. There is nothing worse than seeing a brand which has so many artistic filters and frills that it looks great on a website but is illegible and commercially unviable to reproduce on a billboard or vehicle. A commercially aware designer should evaluate the range of visual mediums you use within your company and provide a design that will meet the practical needs of the company as it grows or diversifies.

A great exercise in the 3 second visibility test;
On approaching or passing a motorway service station which brands are instantly recognisable and legible on the haulage vehicles? Alternatively when you approach your out of town shopping mall which billboards can you read and identify first? What colour, font, shape or symbols are most visible and legible?

Colour
Because colour is the 1st thing we visually register it is essential that you take careful consideration to your choice of company colours. Colour is one of the most important decisions in branding because it will be used for your uniform selection process, interior design, signage, vehicles, marketing literature etc. This is why I advise that it is essential that companies should take professional advice to avoid costly mistakes when creating their brand.

When choosing colours you have to ask what do you associate, feel, rationalise, and relate to with this colour or colour combination. Your colour selection of brand and uniform colours are so important because colour communicates and generates various emotive responses and reactions. It can influence the emotions and moods of its wearer and generate different subconscious reactions and responses from the observer.

Symbolism & Styling

Your choice of symbolism and styling is also conveyed through your choice of font, logo shape, artistic styling & filters each impacting on your message as a brand. A font alone can communicate a variety of messages from its casing, contrasts of colour, italics, size and scale. Something as simple as your choice of font can communicate and define you as a modern, traditional or creative company.

Summary

Principle Four; the visual representation of your business starts with your company brand, it is the template for every other visual element of your business.

Principle Five: The essential ingredients to a successful brand are; name, visibility, colour, styling.

Chapter 3

Colour

Colour is the 1st thing we visually register when we meet someone, yet most individuals lack the understanding and confidence to use colour as one of the most powerful tools in creating their personal or corporate image. Throughout this book we will provide practical tools which will help you choose colours which will enhance your image and make the investment in your personal and corporate image more profitable. Chapters 6, 7, 9 & 10 discuss the benefits of how to use colour effectively with "Colour analysis", "Accessorise" & "Corporate Wardrobe".

Principle Six; Colour is the one essential visual tool in "How to Dress for Business"

There are various considerations when choosing your uniform colour palette it must also take into account:
- Colour availability; colour matching, accessorising.
- Conflicts; Fashionability, likability, negative associations, regional colours based on football alliances.
- Cultural & religious associations or taboos.

- Traditions within Professional roles

- Competitor; conflicts of identity.

- Differentiate; Level of distinction, originality and visibility.

Colour availability

Fortunately most reputable uniform manufacturers produce uniforms in colours and fabrics which unlike the Fashion industry change every season they have stock supported ranges which last for 2 to 6 years plus, which ensures stock continuity and that your image can be maintained over a 2 to 4 year period.

Over the years I have had customers who have had bad experiences with uniform suppliers where they were advised on a very distinct and unusual colour for their suiting and main corporate colour. Only to be advised a month later that this colour of suiting was being discontinued because the colour was no longer being woven for suiting fabrics. Consequently they could not source any stock supported or made to order garments in that colour to either supplement the existing uniforms or provide uniforms for any new members of staff.

Conflicts

It would amaze you the different reactions I have received over the years simply because of colour. Issues from the choice of uniform and accessory colours and their similarity to rival football team colours.

Cultural & Religious associations

If you are an international company you must consider the cultural associations of colour to that culture & region. In the west black is traditionally an associated colour for mourning, where as in India it is white.

Traditions

In many traditional roles the consumer expects to see i.e. the legal, banking & financial professionals dressed in navy pinstripe suits and the medical professionals in white tunics and lab coats.

Competitors

It is essential that your design and marketing team are aware of your competitor's colours and ensure your organisation is distinguishable as a unique brand.

Differentiate

Within roles of safety and security visible colours like your hi-visibility yellows and oranges are essential.

Uniform palette

Your uniform palette should interpret your brand colours into a functional and practical range of clothing colours which include a:

- Base Colour: Dark to Medium neutral colour; for Suiting's, Trousers, Skirts, Dresses, Fleeces, Jacket's.
- Light Colour: Light or Pastel colour; for Shirts, Blouses, Polo-shirts, T-Shirts.
- Accent Colour: Bright colour; for your corporate statement-Ties, Scarves, Textile prints, Polo-shirts, Blouses, Shirts.
- Alternative Colour: Metallic or Neutral colour; for buttons, buckles, trimmings etc. or alternative garment basics.

Principle Seven; What do we all remember? "Colour".

For decades stylists and image consultants have understood how to use colour strategically. The biggest secret is the answer to this question.

What do people notice first, visually register and what do they remember? Colour, the secret ingredient is a memorable colour, an unusual colour or colour combination.

What company do you associate with brown, orange or red?

UPS

Why is UPS such a unique brand because no one else wears brown uniforms & communicate a message that they are safe, trusting & reliable and clearly differentiate themselves from everyone else.

Easy Jet

Orange says cheap, affordable and budget.

Virgin

Red is assertive, energetic, exciting and sexy.

For any company but most importantly for the small company trying to compete with the big boys the secret is people rarely remember the details of the dark, neutral or dull coloured stock supported suit in black or navy.

They remember and recall that bright accent brand colour used in that unusual Corporate Tie & Scarf or that bright coloured blouse or shirt.

To build a suit of armour and dress for business start by taking the cheapest component of a uniform your accessories; ties, scarves, badges and use it to display your brand. Choose a selection of garments i.e. suit, trousers, blouses, shirts in dark or light neutrals and accentuate and differentiate them with a bright Tie or Scarf from your "Brand palette".

The simple Tie or Scarf can be the focal point and key element to your uniform. Many small companies who don't have the budget or resources to provide a uniform will ask staff to agree on a general dress code and agree to wear black suiting and white shirts and blouses or navy suiting and white shirts of their own, while the company supplies a bright personalised company tie & scarf.

The same principle is used with large corporations who commission an exclusive textile print which is then produced in patterned blouses and ties to achieve the same effect but at a greater cost and expense to the employer.

Scarves come in 3 shapes; oblong, rectangular and square. The most versatile shape for scarf tying is an oblong shaped scarf 60" x 9" in a light weight voile or silk. A voile or polyester crepe oblong scarf is ideal for corporate wear which can be produced in a full spectrum of shades and customised design.

Like wise you can commission both a printed or woven Tie designs to colour match your scarf design to create a strong corporate image.

Summary

Principle Six; Colour is the one essential visual tool in "How to Dress for Business"

Principle Seven; What do we all remember? "Colour"

Chapter 4

Uniforms & Dress codes

Uniforms & Dress code policies

When we look in further detail to the communication of clothing we look at the subject of uniforms and dress codes. Uniforms and Dress codes are not suitable for all organisations and may be effective within selective departments of an organisation. The decision to implement either should directly correlate to the age, culture and style of your organisation.

Principle Eight; Uniforms and Dress codes are not suitable for all organisations.

A comment from one of Americas leading authors on image and the individual responsible for probably the only extensive survey on 'people's responses to image' in the past 40 years;

"The biggest problems in America is not good Dress codes or Bad Dress Codes, it is umbrella Dress codes which put everyone in the company in the same uniform.'

This quote from over 2 decades ago predicted the decline of one of the worlds leading companies in computer technology where a formal dress code was part of their company mantra.

'Long term; the salvation of IBM and every other high-tech Company in America will depend on innovation in the creation of new products, not just on selling them........IBM is going to have to attract and hold creative people....IBM will have limited success in this area unless they change their image.' with IBM's existing Image students hold the belief that they don't encourage creative people.'

Today we have high-tech industry spear headed by creative student types which have no regard or interest in dress code policies and uniforms. This is an example of one industry which doesn't fit into the uniform mould.

The only single area where there are no exceptions and compromises for any individual or company are in; personal hygiene, cleanliness, tidiness and grooming. Whether you are the biggest and most successful professional or free thinking organisation in the world nothing excuses or makes exceptions for two things:

1. *Good personal dental, hair and hygiene care and grooming.*
2. *Tidy, Repaired, Ironed and clean clothing.*

The decision to implement a uniform must be well thought through in the context of your staff, your business culture, ethos, customer's needs, expectations and motivations. Ultimately you understand your business better than anyone you must ultimately decide what culture you wish to create.

Questions to ask:

- How big is your company today and how big will it be in the future?
- What do you want to develop inside your company?
- What is your company culture and what type of atmosphere do you need for staff to work productively and positively?
- Is there a need for uniformity or individuality?
- What are the needs of different departments, individuals, age, sex, work culture?
- Is there different levels of workforce with different needs; images of authority, team work, superiority, disassociation with staff team image?
- Who could be your prospective employee: temporary employees, young people in first time employment, graduates, students etc.
- What type of employee do you wish to attract?
- How do you wish to promote you and your staff to customers?
- What are your customers' needs and expectations?

Corporate Identity and Personal image are two very different subjects. Personal image and identity can be a very emotive issue for many individuals. We always recommend that you evaluate the wants and needs of your employees as equally as your company needs. The mention of a uniform can create extreme emotive reactions from employees often created by misconceptions of what it will involve without rationalising the benefits or disadvantages i.e.

- Fears of intimate details of your clothing size being this week's office gossip.
- Will you be asked to wear unfashionable or inferior quality clothing?
- Your staffs have had an uncomfortable experience with uniforms, from past employers.
- Those memories of school uniforms!

Over the years there have seen many successful examples documented in surveys and reviews on uniforms and their relevance within the British workplace: A survey was completed from a sample of 641 organisations with secretarial and office staff; 13 specialist divisions, over 200 branches throughout the country. By Personnel Services, Reed Employment summary report 11th April 1996.

'' 70% of employees believed that some form of dress code (whether a uniform or smart casuals) was the best option to enhance staff morale and productivity''.

This general accord is misleading. It seems that choosing a suitable wardrobe for the workplace has never been so demanding and Reed's survey confirms this. Effects of formality; James Reed Director; Reed Employment

'' People themselves believe that how they dress at work directly affects both how their organisation is viewed from the outside and how, they behave within the workplace.''

"Among employees, uniforms conferred professionalism, encouraged team spirit and even reduced class barriers."

'Employers were keen because uniforms, particularly for front-line staff, were important in giving the right image to the outside world'.

18% only allow their employees wear what ever they want; thumbs down from employers and employees.

13% only argued this as a preferable option. Responses; *"Individuality leads to a relaxed staff; communicating an organisation has 'Informal cultural values'.*

Your aim is to build a corporate look for customers that inspire confidence in your company's staff, products & services while providing work wear or business wear which meets staff needs and expectations that you can maintain and sustain.

Many modern organisations have either a relaxed no-dress code policy, or a strict to moderate corporate uniform or dress code policy or both. Dress code policies vary in detail from strict Airline codes of dress to simple professional codes of practice.

Principle Nine; Only implement a Company Uniforms if you have the resources to sustain, maintain a quality uniform that improves your staffs confidence and credibility.

In the case of large corporations it is always advisable to complete an initial survey with 10% of your staff, and then request a small group of staff to participate in a 4 month wearer trial. This should be followed with a second questionnaire for trial wearers, and opinions gathered from colleagues and customers about its effectiveness before deciding to have a final roll out of uniforms.

In the past the provision of clothing supplied by an employer constitutes a taxable benefit out with the exception of the general rules that; *The clothing is genuinely protective clothing worn as a matter of physical necessity because of the nature of the job this covers items such as overalls, protective gloves, footwear etc.*

The clothing is recognisable as a uniform or part of a uniform and the employee is required as part of his or her duties, to wear it. It is not sufficient that clothing is described as a uniform in the sense that all the employees of a particular group wear the same item. If any employer requires his or her employees to wear blue lounge suits of the same style, they would not thereby become "a uniform" they would remain, ordinary civilian clothing.

The test being whether someone wearing the clothing would be recognisable in the street as wearing a uniform in the same way as one would identify a police officer, nurse or doctor.

Applying permanent embroidery, badges or tax-tabs may be sufficient but always discuss this with your local Inland Revenue Office. Keep up to date and be aware of the latest guidelines and rules related to uniforms and the differences of being sometimes considered "a taxable gift in kind" and not always a uniform.

Please take advice from your own HR department when implementing or updating your own dress code policy to be aware of the latest legislative rules for employers and employees i.e. Religious dress, health and safety at work, tax allowances.

Summary

Principle Eight; Uniforms and Dress codes are not suitable for all organisations

Principle Nine; Only implement a Company Uniforms if you have the resources to sustain, maintain a quality uniform that improves your staffs confidence and credibility.

Chapter 5

Uniform Supplier

When selecting a uniform supplier it is essential that you are confident that the supplier can provide a full compliment of services to ensure the efficient implementation of staff uniforms i.e. fittings, alterations, embroidery, tax-tabbing, and individual bagging. Always request references and testimonials of contracts and tenders supplied to other organisations and companies.

It is essential to obtain a supplier who will provide:

1. A courteous and confidential service; where staffs individual sizing remains confidential.
2. Fitting staff on site to complete supervised fittings.
3. A full compliment of sizes and styles for fitting
4. Provide items which are consistent in quality and sizing.
5. A range of sizes and lengths for all age groups of staff i.e. longer length skirts, less tapered styled jackets.
6. Products which will still be available in your choice of colour, fabric and styling 2-3 years from date of initial purchase.

7. Professional staff with expertise and experience in tailoring / fitting male & female staff, and skills in providing alterations.

8. The services to meet all your staff needs and ensure every member of staff is accommodated with the equivalent uniform; ladies wear sizes 24+, menswear 48"+, maternity wear, adjustments and alterations for disabled members of staff.

A reputable supplier will provide a cross range of samples to preview and evaluate and advise on style and quality of items relevant to your budget and term of renewal. A reputable supplier will provide optional suiting lengths for both petite and tall fittings and stock supported items for women sized 6 to 24/26 and men's trousers 28" to 44" / Suit Jackets 34" to 50". A reputable tailor will provide a full fitting service to ensure garments are delivered to the correct size, length and fit and should advise on any necessary preparations.

Principle Ten; Ensure that your uniform supplier will provide a professional service that protects and respects individual staff confidentiality.

Fittings can be a very emotive experience for individuals for a mixture of personal reasons. It is essential that any uniform supplier can demonstrate systems and procedures where due care is taken to protect staffs personal sizing and fitting information.

Over the years my aim was always to provide quality products that improved staff self esteem and a service that was sensitive to the needs of each member of staff and promoted staff confidentiality. From the hundred of individuals I have fitted over the years I have a true understanding of the frailties and insecurities of people.
We live in a society where many individuals have real challenges with their body weight and self image which can become magnified when focused on in the work place.

Over the years my work has taken me into people's confidence, where they have shared their personal challenges with their self image dealing with the results of cancer with hair loss, a mastectomy to the challenges of weight loss, eating disorders and issues of low self esteem. I have learned never to make assumptions or judgements about peoples level's of confidence or self esteem on size, body shape, weight and self image. I have had countless occasions where I have been introduced to a member of staff for the first time for fittings and can see the worry and anguish in their face because they are going to have to discuss with me their clothing size. On a personal note it is essential that any uniform supplier can demonstrate systems and procedures where due care and respect is taken to protect staffs personal sizing and fitting information.

To ensure that uniforms are fitted correctly in size, length and fit it is essential that staff prepare for fittings and attend fittings with:

a) Chosen colour of; shoes, tights/ socks and undergarments to be worn with new uniform.

b) A pair of shoes; in the style and height to be worn with uniform; footwear for during summer/ winter.

c) Wear minimum makeup; to avoid marking sample goods.

d) Wear well fitting & supportive undergarments or alternatively wear; Ladies; Leotard & tights or body & leggings. Gents; T-shirt & tracksuit trousers.

Summary

Principle Ten; Ensure that your uniform supplier will provide a professional service that protects and respects individual staff confidentiality.

Chapter 6

Personal & Professional Image

From the employee perspective when joining any new organisation you should always look closely at your contract of employment and the details related to the terms set out under dress code or uniforms. Always evaluate the standard of design and quality of uniform being provided by the company to ensure it enhances your professional image and credibility. Ensure that any dress code is not in conflict with any of your personal or religious values and provides a positive contribution to your professional image and opportunities of advancement.

Principle Eleven; Never agree to a uniform that devalues your professional image or credibility.

'....Women's uniforms can destroy the wearer's authority and credibility. This is particularly destructive since one of the main problems women face in business is being taken seriously. Wearing feminine uniforms, your employees will have a great deal of difficulty handling customers, particularly in an emergency, situation or if the customer is upset.....the wrong uniform can destroy a woman's effectiveness and the effectiveness of the entire organisation.'

Dress codes and uniforms are considered a favourable choice by employees within the U.K. Unfortunately on occasion companies can get uniforms wrong. Always ensure your new employer has a uniform that is modern, fit for purpose and enhances your self confidence and authority.

''Wearing the Correct outfit makes the wearer appear more confident, puts them into ' work-mode'- making them instinctively think and act more clearly- enhances the job and lends an air of professionalism. And in a school, a uniform is a type of discipline.''

''One in 2 people in Britain now go to work wearing a Co. Uniform- this totals over 32 million garments per year.'' Vermillion Corporate wear

'An executive who decides not to wear the uniform of his position may still be in the race, but he is carrying extra weight and although he or she may win they are working against a needless disadvantage.'

It is self evident that women are more heavily scrutinised about image than men, and are unfairly disadvantaged in many sectors if they have a poor image that does not reflect their professional role.

''Women who wear makeup can expect to earn 12 to 15 % more than women who don't.''

''1/3 rd of the problems associated with women breaking the glass ceiling in senior management has been associated with Image.''

'' Margaret Thatcher learned the value of being well groomed and dressed for the job; allowed her to confidently forget about her appearance and get on with the work at hand.''

From the employee perspective within a company without a dress code or uniform or with a role where uniforms are irrelevant there are a variety of tools which can help you improve your image and opportunities for professional advancement.

Colour analysis

One of the most helpful tools in establishing your personal or professional image is colour analysis. Colour analysis is a formula for evaluating which colours are the most flattering and enhancing to you as an individual.

The system of colour analysis can be over simplified as a system of 4 colour categories named spring, summer, autumn and winter. A spring or autumn category is for individuals with an overall dominant warm orange based colouring in their skin, hair and eye colours. A summer or winter category is for individuals with an overall dominant cool blue based colouring in their skin, hair and eye colours.

This is expanded further into more defined categorise which defines a range of colours which are most complimentary to your individual colouring. A professional image consultant and colour analyst can perform this evaluation and will complete the evaluation by providing you with a personalised wallet or palette of fabric colours which you can use when shopping and selecting colours. This is an excellent tool to give you confidence to;

- Experiment with colours that are guaranteed to be flattering to your individual appearance.
- Build a long term wardrobe of colours, rather than a fashion wardrobe that dates.
- Invest in quality garments rather than fad fashion colours.
- Save valuable time and money by making good colour purchases.
- Build a wardrobe of items that co-ordinate and mix and match.

Summary

Principle Eleven; Never agree to a uniform that devalues your professional image or credibility.

Part Two

Chapter 7

Colour

Colour communicates and generates various emotive responses and reactions. It can influence the emotions and moods of its wearer and generate different subconscious reactions and responses from the observer. Your choice of brand colour and uniform colour is one of the most important decisions in the uniform selection process.

Colour	Contrast	Emotions +	Emotions -	Image +	Image -	Industry
Red	Indigo	Confident	Stressed	Assertive	Aggressive	Entertainment
Blue	Magenta	Relaxed	Cold	Trustworthy	Predictable	Customer service
Green	Orange	Self control	Boring	Self reliant	Predictable	Environmental
Yellow	Purple	Optimistic	Excitable	Sociable	Cowardly	Technology
Magenta	Blue	Passion	Impulsive	Assertive	Feminine	Female market
Indigo	Red	Fearless	Negative	Powerful	Fearful	Services - authority
Orange	Blue	Enthusiastic	Giddy	Sociable	Common	Sports
Purple	Yellow	Creative	Depressed	Spiritual	Superior	Spiritual
White	Black	Innocence	Naive	Clinical	Sterile	Clinical
Black	White	Confident	Depressed	Strong	Authoritative	Police, Magistrate
Grey	Ivory	Serious	Boring	Respectable	Safe	Legal, Establishment
Brown	Green	Comfort	Boring	Approachable	unsophisticated	Security

In this chapter we provide a small glimpse at some basic colour associations and the different colour combinations and what they communicate as a look or as accessories.

The conscious and subconscious reactions to colour are be based on the colour, it's depth, intensity and the other colours co-ordinated with it to create a look or brand. For example:

Power Dressing

To appear authoritative & domineering wear; dark suit, white shirt/blouse & red tie or scarf as an accent.

Sales

To appear approachable & friendly, wear; Blues, medium to light tones; medium navy blue or grey coloured suit, baby blue shirt or blouse, royal blue, white & silver tie or scarf & accessories.

Before deciding on your uniform colours it is always advisable to complete an initial survey with 10% of your staff, and then request a small group of staff to participate in a wearer trial. This should be followed with a second questionnaire for trial wearers, and opinions gathered from colleagues and customers about its effectiveness before deciding to have a final roll out of uniforms

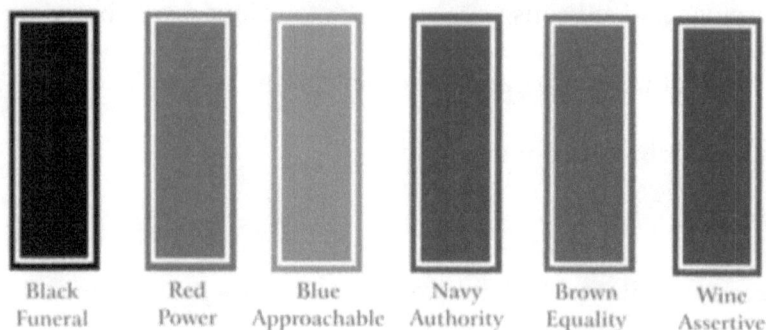

| Black | Red | Blue | Navy | Brown | Wine |
| Funeral | Power | Approachable | Authority | Equality | Assertive |

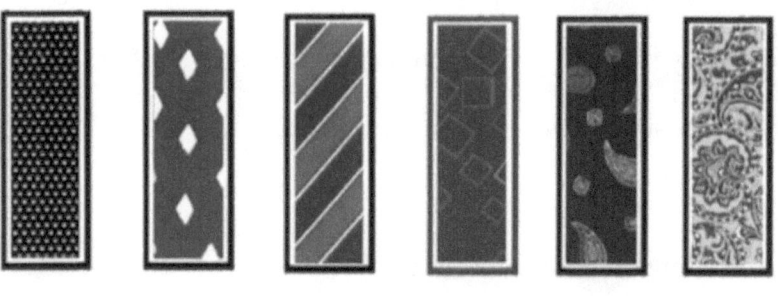

| Small Polka Dot | Diamond | Stripe | Geometrics | Classic Paisley | Traditional |
| Authorative | Elite Club | Conservative | Fashionable | Not Serious | Creative |

SCARVES

TIES

Authoritative Power Dress
Suit: Dark Navy
Blouse: White
Scarf: Red

Assertive Confident
Suit: Dark Navy
Blouse: Baby Blue
Scarf: Dark Navy

Trustworthy Reliable
Suit: Fine Dark Grey Pinstripe
Blouse: Baby Blue

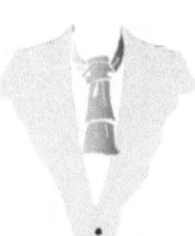

Authoritative Business like
Suit: Fine Dark Navy Pinstripe
Blouse: White
Scarf: Red/ fine pattern

Reliable Conservative
Suit: Dark Grey
Blouse: Baby Blue

Approachable Friendly
Suit: Light Grey
Blouse: Cream
Scarf: Blue

Mature Reliable
Suit: Dark Brown
Blouse: White
Scarf: Gold/Patterned

Creative Informal
Suit: Beige
Blouse: Gold

Casual Relaxed
Suit: Taupe
Blouse: Cream
Scarf: Gold

Authoritative
Power Dress
Suit: Dark Navy
Shirt: White
Tie: Red

Assertive
Confident
Suit: Dark Navy
Shirt: Baby Blue
Tie: Dark Navy

Trustworthy
Reliable
Suit: Fine Dark Grey Pinstripe
Shirt: Baby Blue
Tie: Dark Navy

Authoritative
Business like
Suit: Fine Dark Navy Pinstripe
Shirt: White
Tie: Red/ White fine pattern

Reliable
Conservative
Suit: Dark Grey
Shirt: Baby Blue
Tie: Dark Grey

Approachable
Friendly
Suit: Light Grey
Shirt: Blue
Tie: Navy

Mature
Reliable
Suit: Dark Navy
Shirt: White
Tie: Gold/Patterned

Creative
Informal
Suit: Beige
Shirt: Lilac
Tie: Purple mix pattern

Casual
Relaxed
Suit: Taupe
Shirt: Cream
Tie: Gold

Chapter 8

Uniforms & Dresscodes

As discussed previously Uniforms and Dress codes are not suitable for all organisations. The decision to implement either should take into consideration employee's views and opinions. Here are a few questions which you may ask to evaluate staff opinions on implementing a uniform or dress code.

Staff Questionnaires

- Do you think corporate wear is a good idea?..........
- Have you ever had a corporate uniform before?...........
- If yes, what was your experience of having a uniform?..........
- Which style of garment do you prefer for work?...................
- What colour of uniform would you like?.....................
- Do you believe a uniform should be compulsory?..................
- How much do you spend on clothing for work each year?..........
- Which public corporate wear uniforms do you like and why?.................
- Do you have any specific clothing needs or concerns for work.....................
- Would you be willing to purchase selected items i.e. your blouses?..........

- Who would you like to nominate as your Dept. representative for Corporate wear decisions?.....
- Questions:...............
- Comments:............

Dress Code samples

In Chapter 7 & 8 we have examples of a general Dress code policy and an Airline dress code policy. *We have included these extreme examples to demonstrate that in certain occupations it is very important to establish an authoritative and disciplined image.*

These are used merely as an example where you can use components to discuss with your HR department how you wish to design your own dress code policy. Please note that these examples do not reflect many of the changes implemented in the past ten years with the challenges made by employees with regards to "Self expression". While equally no viable studies or research has been provided in over 30 years on the change in cultural attitudes and diversity to dress code and its impact on business & customer perception or staff moral.

These examples demonstrate how both men and women for e.g. in the Airline industry must instil confidence and authority to enforce safety and security measures. Similarly in policing, the military and security services image is a major communications tool for enforcing authority and conveying confidence. (Extracts from leading UK Airline Dress codes)

General Dress Code Policy

(Sample 1)

Introduction

Having made this valuable investment in your Corporate Uniform only you can complete the Corporate Uniform and Image. It is vital that you carefully consider the enclosed details.

Some comments may seem like common sense however worthwhile some consideration and attention. Please feel free to discuss with us any recommendations which feel too personally inhibiting or conflict with any of your religious beliefs. The recommendations aim to ensure the execution of a successful Professional Image in the workplace.

All recommendations are key elements in; creating & maintaining your companies' corporate image and assist you in your career advancement within your organisation.

The Golden rules for maintaining your Corporate Business wear & Image;

1. Colour; Keep to our corporate colour scheme and colours.

2. Clothing; consider & practice suggestions on; accessorising, security, home care, cleaning instructions & stain removal.

3. Grooming; the small details.

Groups of staff when working together must maintain a uniform appearance. All staff must confer on which items must be worn for any Promotional Activities.

Personal Hygiene

Antiperspirant / deodorant must be used to prevent body odour and form part of your locker kit.

Dental Hygiene is essential, breath freshener to be used when appropriate; avoid eating spicy foods before work. Hair must always be clean and nails must be well manicured and clean.

Hair styles & Grooming

Grooming is a vital element of your complete Professional Image the following will seem like common sense however worthwhile some attention and consideration.

Staff handling food or drink or machinery, must observe extreme care regarding length of hair and personal hygiene.

Hair should not to be combed or styled in front of customers.

Hair which falls onto the face when leaning over is not acceptable.

Hair must always be clean.

Gel is permissible but this should not create a 'wet look'.

No outrageous styles and colours are permitted.

No excessive hair accessories i.e. sweat bands, elaborate rosettes, scrunches, combs and slides.

Makeup

Is your own personal choice; but even a touch creates a more healthy and professional appearance.

Do not reapply in front of customers or public.

Nails

Must be well manicured and clean.

False and sculpted nails are permitted but must be well maintained at all times.

Tattoos

Tattoos or Henna body painting should never be visible when in uniform or when representing Company on business.

Piercing

No visible body piercing. No studs are permitted or any other visible body piercing, whilst on representing company during business occasions, conferences and exhibitions, external training.

Men's Hair

Hair must be clean and neatly styled so that it remains in place whilst working. Fringe must not fall over eye brows/ eyes. If tinted it must be regularly maintained in a natural looking shade. Obvious dark roots and streaks or shading are not acceptable re-growth must not be visible.
No severely shaved and graded hairstyles, sideburns or crew cuts. Tinted and highlighted hair must tone in with natural colour.

Toupees

Permitted at management discretion and as long as they adhere to hair regulations. Must be indistinguishable, well groomed and securely fitted and of a natural colour.

Beards & Moustache

Must be neatly trimmed and groomed. A clean shaven appearance is required.

Turban

When the wearing of a turban has been agreed it must be white or navy.

Hands

Must appear well cared for and manicured

Security

You have responsibility to take care of all Company Property.

You must avoid leaving your corporate uniform in i.e. car.

Any stolen uniform items must be reported to a senior member of staff.

Your uniform or any item, shall not be sold, loaned or given to individuals not authorised to wear it. Any replacement item may be charged for. Avoid wearing Uniform out with hours of work to maintain appearance and life of garments.

On termination of employment the uniform must be returned, cleaned, pressed and in good repair. No alterations may be carried out without written permission from senior management.

Security Pass

Must be worn at all times when on duty.

All ID holders or chains worn should be corporate issue.

The ID pass should be worn on a Corp. Chain around the neck or clipped squarely to the right lapel opposite the name badge.

Badges

The following are badges that may be worn with the uniform:

- Name Badge
- Brevet
- First Aid Badge
- Sign Language
- Hard of hearing/profoundly deaf badge

The information displayed on the name badge must comply with one:

First Name & Surname e.g. Katherine Brown

Known name & Surname-Kate Brown

1st Name-Katherine

Known Name-Kate

1st Name, 2nd initial-Katherine M Brown

Initials Co Directors/ Mgrs & Supervisory

Staff badges must display 1st Name or Known Name, Surname & Position. If you are wearing a blouse or shirt on its own you must display your name badge. ID Badges; Poppies etc. may be worn at the appropriate time of year.

Women's Uniform

General Dress Code Policy (Sample 1)

Jackets & Blazers

Jackets & Blazers must be worn when dealing with the public.

Store on hanger, when not in use; avoid hanging on backs of chairs and clothes hooks. If jacket is not worn, it should be folded and carried over arm, never draped over shoulders. Not to be rolled up or placed over bag etc. Avoid over filling pockets, and using outside pockets. Collar may not be worn turned up. To be worn with Company scarf or cravat.

Shirt or Blouse

To be worn buttoned up at all times. Pocket must not be overfilled.

Skirt

To be worn no shorter than 1" above knee bone.

Coat

Collar can be worn up or down. If not worn coat should be folded and carried over arm. Must not be rolled up and placed in strap of bag etc. Pockets must not be overfilled.

Cardigan

Only uniform cardigan may be worn. Store on hanger or folded on clothing shelves, when not in use; avoid hanging on backs of chairs and clothes hooks.

Hosiery

Recommended; Navy or natural or opaque and must not have patterns or seams. Hosiery must be worn at all times. If profession demands frequently standing; choose support tights or stockings.

Underwear

Quote by renowned Designer; "Without under garments there is no fashion". A complimenting coloured camisole or bra must always be worn with light coloured blouses (no dark or bright coloured underwear under light blouses).

Accessories

Shoes

Must at all times be clean, well polished and maintained in a good state of repair. The design should be classic in style. Platform soles are not permitted.

Recommended height for safety & comfort less than 2"

Loafers/lace up not permitted.

Boots

Must only be worn at appropriate times of year.

Suede, patent or patterned boots are not acceptable.

Avoid wearing with knee length skirts.

Contact Lenses

Must be of the wearers natural eye colour or clear.

Earrings

Only one pair of earrings may be worn, with one earring in each ear.

Nose studs and sleepers must not be worn with the uniform.

Rings

Rings are not to be worn on thumb or index finger, avoid large fashion rings. No ankle chains.

Men's Uniform

General Dress Code Policy (Sample 2)

Jackets & Blazers

When dealing with the public must be available to wear.

If jacket is not worn, it should be folded and carried over arm, never draped over shoulders or rolled up or placed over bags etc. Do not over fill pockets, avoid using outside pockets. Collar may not be worn turned up. Always wear jacket, when wearing a short sleeved shirt & dealing with the public.

Trousers

To be worn with belt at all times. Contents of pockets must not distort the shape of trousers, no adornments i.e. unusual buckles etc.

Shirt

To be worn buttoned up and tucked inside trousers at all times.

Collar must always be buttoned down. Tie must always be worn with shirt. Shirts with long sleeves must be fastened at the wrists, not rolled or pushed up. If necessary the pocket must only contain a pen and may be used to attach the ID pass with the corporate issue chain or clip.

Coat

Collar can be worn up or down.

When not worn coat should be folded and carried over arm.

Must not be rolled up and placed in strap of bag etc.

Tie

A tie must always be worn with a shirt with the back of the tie placed through loop on tie. Avoid wearing Tie pins & bars. The tip of the tie must touch the top of the belt buckle.

Pullover

Only uniform pullover may be worn.

Shoes

Shoes are acceptable in 2 styles; Classic Lace-up's or high fronted slip on which do not reveal socks. Excessively thick soled shoes are not acceptable. Shoes must be clean, well polished and maintained in a good state of repair at all times. Shoes should primarily be comfortable and co-ordinated with suit and sock colour.

Socks

Plain dark colours are acceptable.

Rings

Must not be worn on index finger or thumb, no more than 2 rings maximum, of a plain design.

The medic alert bracelet is the only bracelet permitted. No neck chains or earrings.

Airline

Dress Code Policy (Sample 1)

Introduction

Employees must be clearly identifiable at all times by customers for safety and security. Uniformity of appearance must be maintained at all times. Groups of staff when working together must maintain a uniform appearance. All staff must confer on which items must be worn for any Promotional Activities.

Security

You have responsibility to take care of all Company Property.

You must not leave your uniform in i.e. car.

Any stolen uniform items must be reported to a senior member of staff and reported to the Police.

Your uniform or any item, shall not be sold, loaned or given to individuals not authorised to wear it.

Any replacement items may be charged for.

Avoid wearing Uniform out with hours of work to maintain appearance and life of garments.

On termination of employment uniforms must be returned, cleaned, pressed and in a good state of repair.

No alterations may be carried out without written permission from senior management.

Security Pass

Must be worn at all times when on duty.

All ID holders or chains worn should be corporate issue.

The ID pass should be worn on a Corp. Chain around the neck or clipped squarely to the right lapel opposite the name badge & brevet.

Badges

The following are badges that may be worn with the uniform:

- Name Badge
- Brevet
- First Aid Badge
- Sign Language
- Hard of hearing/profoundly deaf badge

The information displayed on the name badge must comply with one:

First Name & Surname- e.g. Katherine Brown

Known name & Surname-Kate Brown

1st Name-Katherine

Known Name-Kate

1st Name, 2nd initial-Katherine M Brown

Initials Co Directors/ Mgrs & Supervisory

Staff badges must display 1st Name or Known Name, Surname & Position.

If you are wearing a blouse or shirt on its own you must display your name badge. ID Badges; Poppies etc. may be worn at the appropriate time of year.

Hair styles & Grooming

Grooming is a vital element of your complete Professional Image the following will seem like common sense however worthwhile some attention and consideration. Staff handling food or drink or machinery, must observe extreme care regarding length of hair and personal hygiene.

Personal Hygiene

Antiperspirant/ deodorant must be used to prevent body or foot odour & form part of your locker kit.

Dental Hygiene is essential, breath freshener to be used when appropriate avoid eating spicy foods.

Hair must always be clean and nails must be well manicured and clean.

No excessive perfume.

Posture

Poor posture can create the uneven drape of clothing appearing untidy and unprofessional.

Avoid; slouching, crossed or folded arms, putting your hands in your pockets.

Sit comfortable, back and shoulders relaxed and straight.

Hair

Hair Length

Hair must always be clean.

Gel is permissible but this should not create a 'wet look'.

Tinted and highlighted hair must tone in with natural colour and re-growth must not be visible.

Fringe must not fall over eye brows/ eyes.

When hair is worn loose it must not fall more than 2.5cm (1") below the neckline of the jacket. Pony tail, single plait, single braid, french braid, bun, twist or roll no longer than 8" falling centrally and neatly or must not drop more than 12.5cm (5"), from the neckline of the jacket secured with only one of the specified accessories. If grips or bands are used they should be concealed. Slides and combs; must be plain design no bigger than ½" (25mm) wide & ¼" (6mm) deep.

Alice bands no bigger than ½" (12mm) wide, must not be worn with any other hair accessory. When hair is tied back, only one company ruffle to be worn. No more than 3 combs/ slides to be worn, these should be tortoiseshell only. If a hair net is used over a bun, it must be extremely fine and of the same colour as the hair. Scrunches, Ribbons and Bows: Must be plain, velvet, satin, plain matte or cross grain ribbon, no wider than 1" (25mm) wide. Bows must be no wider than 4" (100mm) used only to secure, ponytail, plait, or braid. Only one scrunchie, ribbon or bow, may be worn.

Not acceptable:

Excessively teased, back combed styles and the use of elaborate hairstyles which look unnatural.

Spiky, gelled, wet look and close shaven hairstyles.

Hair which falls onto the face when leaning over.

Hair should not to be combed or styled in front of customers.

No frizzy perms or outrageous styles and colours are permitted.

Sweat bands, elaborate rosettes, scrunches, combs and slides are not acceptable; no other hair ornaments other than those specified are acceptable.

Hair Extensions: are not permitted.

Makeup

Is your own personal choice; but even a touch of makeup creates a more healthy and professional appearance. Makeup must be checked at regular intervals and reapplied when necessary, but not in front of customers or public. Makeup should be a colour complimentary to uniform and own personal colouring. Facial tinted moisturisers are permitted. Foundation, blusher, lipstick and mascara must always be part of your makeup routine. Eyebrows must be kept neatly in shape; must not be shaved. Mascara must be either black or brown. False eyelashes are not permitted.

Nails

Must be well manicured and clean; if painted; choose clear or coloured manicure, in a complimentary colour to the lipstick being worn.
False and sculpted nails are permitted but must be well maintained at all times.

Skin care

Dermatologists insist that great skin is possible for everyone. What it takes is an understanding of what skin is going through at any one time.

Tattoos

Tattoos or Henna body painting should never be visible when in uniform or when representing Company.

Piercing

No visible body piercing. No studs are permitted or any other visible body piercing, whilst on duty including Company social and business occasions, conferences and exhibitions, external training.

Men's Hair

Must be clean and neatly styled so that it remains in place whilst working, it must not touch the shirt collar at the back or sides.

Fringe must not fall over eye brows/ eyes.

Sideburns must be no longer than the earlobe or wider than 1"(25mm).

If tinted it must be regularly maintained in a natural looking shade.

Short hair required but not less than a No. 2 blade.

Not acceptable:

Obvious dark roots and streaks or shading are not acceptable re-growth must not be visible.

Severely shaved and graded hairstyles, including crew cuts and flat tops, which leave the scalp clearly visible are not acceptable.

Tinted and highlighted hair must tone in with natural colour and

Hair should not be worn over the collar of the shirt.

Toupees

Permitted at management discretion and as long as they adhere to hair regulations. Must be indistinguishable well groomed and securely fitted and of a natural colour.

Beards & Moustache

For reasons of safety the wearing of beards by cabin crew is not permitted.

Where the wearing of a beard is approved, it must be neatly trimmed and groomed. Must be neatly groomed and must not extend past the corner of the mouth than ½ "(12.5mm). Outline of top lip must be clearly visible.

Turban

When the wearing of a turban has been agreed it must be white or navy.

Grooming

A clean shaven appearance is required and any superfluous hair i.e. neckline, etc should be well groomed. Obvious blemishes and skin conditions should be concealed wherever possible.

Women's Uniform

Airline Dress Code Policy (Sample 1)

Jackets & Blazers

To be buttoned at all times including inner button except when seated bottom button may be undone.

Jackets must always be worn when dealing with the public.

Store on hanger, when not in use; avoid hanging on backs of chairs and clothes hooks.

If jacket is not worn, it should be folded and carried over arm, never draped over shoulders.

Not to be rolled up or placed over bag etc.

It is recommended that jacket is not worn when driving.

Avoid over filling pockets, and using outside pockets.

Collar may not be worn turned up.

To be worn with Company scarf or cravat at all times.

Blouse

To be worn buttoned up at all times.

Scarf or cravat must always be worn with shirt.

Pocket must not be overfilled.

Skirt

Must be worn with uniform issued belt at all times; passed through belt loops; with no attachments or adornments. Blouse must be worn tucked inside skirt.

To be worn to regulation length; touching centre of kneecap.

Name Badge must be worn on pocket.

Coat

Collar can be worn up or down.

If not worn coat should be folded and carried over arm.

Scarf should be worn inside coat but be visible at the neck.

Must not be rolled up and placed in strap of bag etc.

Pockets must not be overfilled. To be worn buttoned up at all times.

When hood is not in use, fastened underneath or remove from coat.

Cardigan

Only uniform cardigan may be worn. To be buttoned at all times.

Store on hanger or folded on clothing shelves, when not in use; avoid hanging on backs of chairs and clothes hooks. If cardigan is not worn, it should be folded and carried over arm, never draped over shoulders. Not to be rolled up or placed over bag etc. Avoid over filling pockets.

Hosiery

Recommended; Navy or natural or opaque and must not have patterns or seams.

Hosiery must be worn at all times, maximum denier 15.1. Not to be seamed or patterned.

A spare pair should always be carried and kept as stock item in workplace.

If profession demands frequently standing; choose support tights or stockings.

Underwear

Quote by renowned Designer; "Without under garments there is no fashion".

A complimenting coloured camisole or bra must always be worn with a blouse (no dark or bright underwear with light coloured blouses).

All tailored skirt lengths must be a minimum 1" (25mm) below the knee when standing. Long skirt must be worn mid point between ankle & knee.

Accessories

Shoes

Shoes must be clean, well polished and maintained in a good state at all times. Must not be suede or patent without laces, trim or pattern.

The design should be classic court style

Pointed toes, stiletto heels or platform soles are not permitted.

Heel height-measured inside of heel must be between 1"&2"(25-50mm)

Max Recommended height for safety & comfort 2"

Loafers/lace up not permitted.

Boots

Must only be worn with the coat and must not be worn at any other time. Suede or patterned boots are not acceptable. Only wear Boots with trousers; avoid wearing with knee length skirts.

Umbrellas

Should be navy or black and of a business-like appearance.

Wallet / Purse

Must be neat, compact and flat; avoid clutter.

Belts; must be passed through belt loops, co-ordinating with garment, classic and professional.

Classic Navy/Black leather gloves- no other gloves permitted.

Handbag

Do not overfill.

To be kept fastened at all times.

Glasses

Spectacles, if worn must be business-like in appearance i.e. plain framed or unframed glasses of moderate size and design. Acceptable frame colours: black, brown, burgundy, tortoise shell colour, dark blue, silver or gold metal. Sunglasses must not be worn when indoors or when addressing a customer. Tinted optical lenses are acceptable only if the eyes are visible. Suggestion; frames should repeat hair or eye colour; avoid reflective coated lenses if responsibilities include providing seminars and training.

Contact Lenses

Must be of the wearers natural eye colour or clear.

Wrist watches

A Conventional /Classic Designs; Gold, silver or stainless steel finish. Leather strap; brown, black or navy, avoid spring or plastic strapped watches.

Earrings

Earrings must be a single pearl stud no more than 10mm.
Only one pair of earrings may be worn, with one earring in each ear.
Nose studs and sleepers must not be worn with the uniform.

Rings

Rings should be one engagement ring, one wedding and/or eternity ring.
One gold or silver signet or plain dress ring of a moderate design & size.
Rings must not be worn on index finger or thumb, must not be worn on two or more fingers on one hand.
Avoid large fashion rings, no neck chains or necklaces, or ankle chains.

Men's Uniform

Airline Dress Code Policy (Sample 2)

Jackets & Blazers

To be buttoned at all times including inner button except when seated bottom button may be undone. Your jacket must always be available when dealing with the public. If jacket is not worn, it should be folded and carried over arm, never draped over shoulders or rolled up or placed over bags etc. Collar may not be worn turned up. Jacket must not to be worn when driving, do not over fill pockets & avoid using outside pockets. Store on hanger, when not in use; avoid hanging on backs of chairs and clothes hooks. Always wear jacket when wearing a short sleeved shirt & dealing with the public.

Trousers

Must be worn with belt at all times and contents of pockets must not distort the shape of trousers.

You must wear the uniform issued belt at all times, no adornments i.e. unusual buckles etc.

Shirt

To be worn buttoned up at all times with collar buttoned down, tucked inside trousers.

A tie must always be worn with a shirt. Shirts with long sleeves must be fastened at the wrists, not rolled or pushed up. If necessary the pocket must only contain a pen and may be used to attach the ID pass with the corporate issue chain or clip. Pockets must not be filled with cigarettes, notebooks etc.

Coat

Should be buttoned at all times, the collar can be worn up or down. When not worn coat should be folded and carried over arm not rolled up and placed in strap of bag etc. Pockets must not be overfilled.

Scarves may not be worn.

Tie

The tie must always be worn with a shirt with the back of the tie placed through loop on tie. Avoid wearing Tie pins & bars. The tip of the tie must touch the top of the belt buckle. Plain silver or gold tie clips of a moderate size and conventional shape may be worn.

Pullover

Only uniform pullover may be worn. The pullover may not be worn with suit jacket.

Socks

Only plain black or plain dark navy are acceptable.

Shoes

Shoes are acceptable in 2 styles

Classic Lace-up's.

High fronted slip on that does not reveal socks.

No metal, contrasting trim, tassels or extra flaps are permitted. No excessively thick soled shoes.

Shoes must be clean, well polished and maintained in a good state at all times, primarily comfortable and co-ordinated with suit and sock colour.

Rings

You can wear one ring of plain design or one wedding ring.

Rings must not be worn on index finger or thumb.

No more than 2 rings maximum, of a plain design.

Not to be worn on index finger or thumb.

The medic alert bracelet is the only bracelet permitted.

No neck chains or earrings. Wrist watches; Conventional / Classic Designs; Gold, silver or stainless steel finish / Leather strap; brown, black or navy black. Avoid spring or plastic strapped watches.

Chapter 9

Accessorise

Accessorise are an essential component to your uniform and one of the most inexpensive and effective tools for personalising a standard uniform to appear like an exclusively designed uniform.

Your accessories include Ties, Scarves, name badges, embroidery, logo transfers and tax-tabbing. Apply the same principles we have discussed and the rules on colour and combine your brand image or symbol in i.e. the textile print or weave of the Tie or Scarf textile design.

Below are some basic sample Tie & scarf methods of tying to create a variety of different looks. Scarves come in 3 shapes; oblong, rectangular and square. The most versatile shape for scarf tying is an oblong shaped scarf 60" x 9" in a light weight voile or silk.

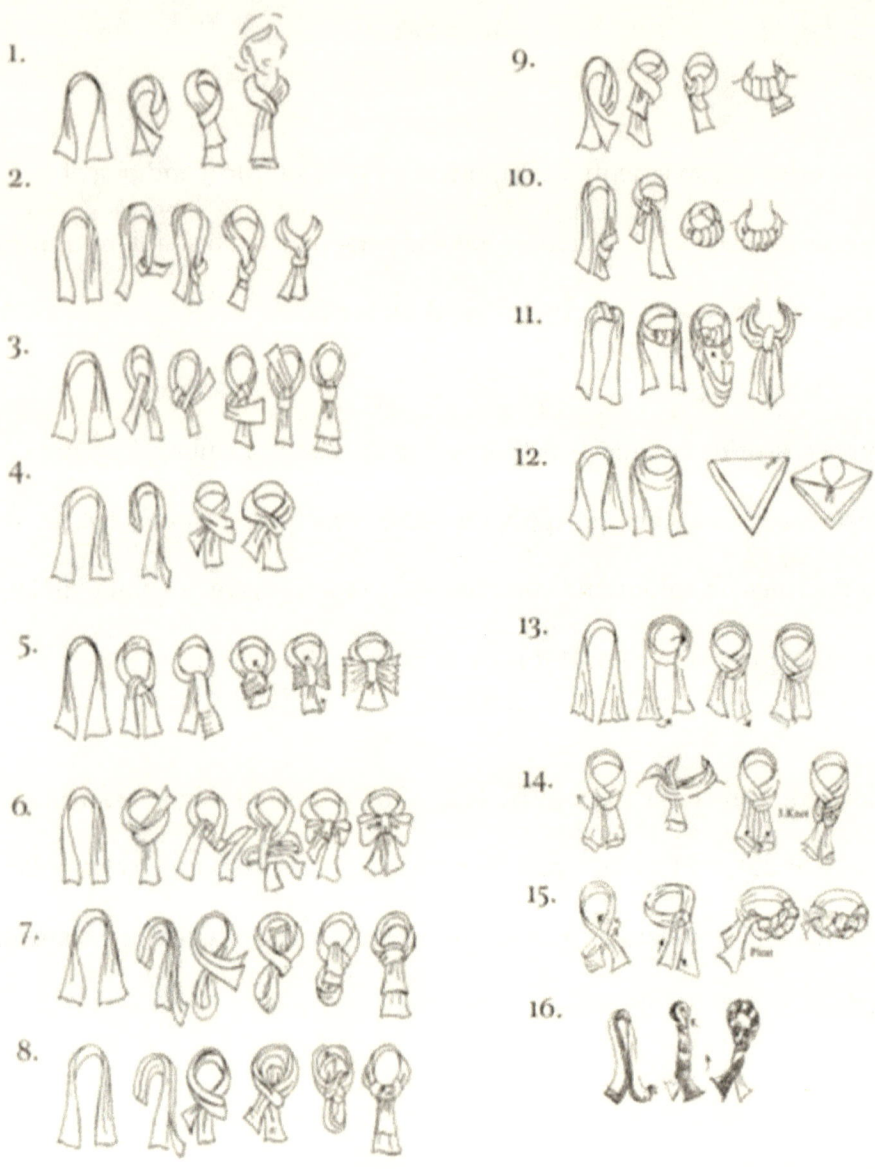

SCARF TYING

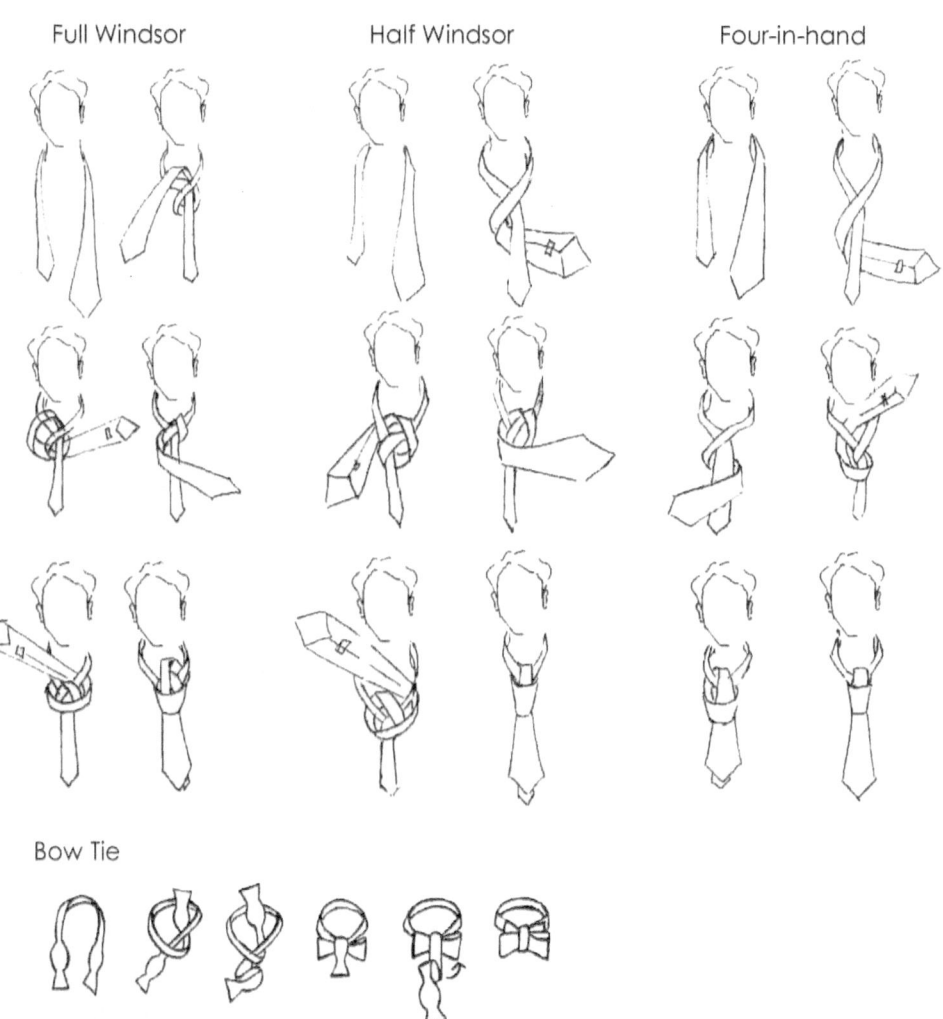

TIE TYING

Chapter 10

The Capsule

A Capsule Uniform is a practical system for co-ordinating and planning your uniform for the short and long term. It allows you to create a lasting, workable and affordable uniform that will be congruent with your brand & identity with the option to update & refresh its image regularly. This is the secret shared by stylists on how to purchase garments intelligently.

The secret to a Capsule Uniform is;

Rule 1: The difference & value between a Classic or Fashionable/ Fad garment or accessory.

Rule 2: How to use Colour.

Rule 3: Capsule equation; how to purchase intelligently and understand the cost per wear or hour.

Rule 1: Classics v Fashion

Classic items: in style and colour your staff could wear 5 years from now. Fashion/Fad items: in style and colour your staff will become tired of and will not want to wear in 1-2 years from now. Classics these are the quality investment items of a uniform, the most expensive:

Items: Suit Jacket, Trouser, Skirt, Dress, Cardigan, Pullover.
Colours: Neutral i.e. Black, White, Cream, Grey, Taupe, Beige, Brown, Wine, Dark Green, Navy, Gold, Silver.
Style: Classic cuts, detailing, lengths & shapes.

Fads these are the lower quality items which require frequent replacing, to add a fresh look to your uniform or simply in the case of shirts and blouses items which naturally have a short life cycle and must be renewed regularly.

Items: Tops, Blouses, Shirts, Scarves & Ties.
Colours: Latest fashion colours, memorable bright colours, vibrant colours; Royal Blue, Gold, Red, Magenta, Turquoise, Orange the accent colours from your corporate branding. Style: Latest blouse style, gent's collar or shape, new cuff or sleeve styling.

Rule 2: How to use Colour

The secret to colours is:

- Understand your corporate brand and stick rigidly to your colour palette. Ensure you have optional colours in a; Dark, Light, and Bright colour.

- What colours will make you instantly recognisable, liked by your customers & be favourable to your staff.

- What colours will be easy to source in uniforms, in complimentary accessories for staff to supply i.e. shoes, hosiery, socks.

- Choose colours which will mix & match with existing items in your existing uniform.

Rule 3: Capsule equation

Remember a Classical designed item of clothing will last 5 years as opposed to a Fashion item which will look dated and no one will wish to wear in 1 year's time.

This equation will assist you in evaluating what to issue as part of a uniform the price, quality & quantity of items, the estimated renewal & replacement period you will have to account for in creating your corporate uniform budget

Item	(Hrs worn)	Days worn	Years	Price item	Cost per hr
Suit Jacket	(1hr)	220	x 2	divided into £60	=14p
Skirt/ Trouser	(8hrs)	220	x 1	divided into £40	=0.023p
Cardigan	(3hrs)	150	x 2	divided into £40	=0.044p
Shirt/Blouse/Polo	(8hrs)	220	x 1	divided into £20	=0.012p
Scarf/Tie	(8hrs)	220	x 2	divided into £10	=0.0029p

No. hrs garment is worn per day x days per yr x No. yrs divided by garment Cost/Price= Cost to employer per hour per uniform garment. This will allow you to rationalise how much to spend on different garments or accessories in your wardrobe. If a suit jacket is simply going to hang on a rail all day replace it with a cardigan.

Women's Capsule: Basic Working Wardrobe

Colours	Dark	Light	Bright
	Navy	Lemon	Red/metallic Gold

1 4-Piece Suit; Jacket, Trousers, Skirt & Waistcoat, 1 Extra Skirt, Shoes, Brief case. (Dark)

1 Sweater crewneck/ 2 Blouses (Light)

3 Scarves, Accessories, 1 Blazer & Skirt. (Bright)

will create 18+ different looks

Plus

1 Trousers, 1 Knitted waistcoat or cardigan; Doubles as Jacket. (Bright)

1 Overcoat, Jeans, T-shirts, Scarf, Hat and Dress. (Lights)

2 Blouses (patterned) (Mix Lights & Brights)

will create 115+ different looks

Men's Capsule: Basic Uniform Capsule

Colours	Dark	Light	Bright
	Black	Pale Blue	Royal Blue/ metallic Gold

1 3-Piece suit Jacket Trousers, W/coat, 1 Extra Trousers, 1 Sweater, Shoes, case, and belt. (Dark)

2 Shirts (Lights)

3 Ties, Handkerchiefs (Brights)

will create 18+ different looks

Plus

1 Blazer & Trousers,+1Trousers, Overcoat, Dress Jacket, 1 Knit w/coat or cardigan. (Darks)

2 Shirts(striped) (Mix Light/Brights) Jeans (Light) (Dress down Friday) T-shirts, Scarf, Tie. (Brights)

will create 115+ different looks

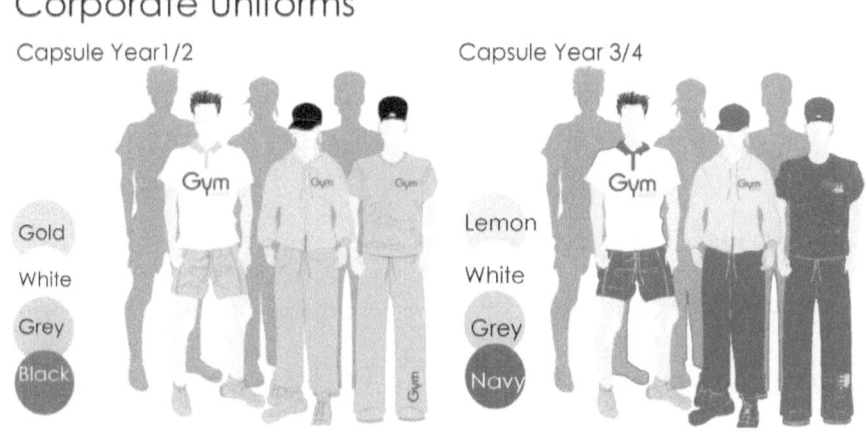

SPORTSWEAR UNIFORM CAPSULE

Chapter 11

Personal Image

The following few chapters looks at issues relevant to your personal and professional image, for those individuals or members of staff where dress codes and uniforms are not applicable i.e. Directors, certain managers, and classifications of self employment.

Please remember that your personal and professional image is equally and if not more important on some occasions than your work force. Your personal or professional image is a reflection of the style of leadership and management in your organisation. "First impressions are created within the 1st 30 seconds of meeting someone, the impression you make is based on; 55% how you look, 38% how you sound and 7% what you actually say."

By understanding image and how to "create your own suit of armour" you can dramatically increase your self confidence and significantly improve your opportunities for employment and career advancement and improve company profitability.

Your professional image should:

Express who you are; your personality, age, lifestyle & tastes through the cut & style of your clothes, your hairstyle & accessories.

Be practical and functional to meet the demands of your job and occupation.

Meet the needs, demands and expectations of customers you serve in your profession.

Your image should communicate an image relative to the value of your products & services i.e. plastic watches, accessories, cheap suiting will create an impression of cheap and disposable services and products.

Aim to be the 'Image' of the post above your present occupation or desired 'Role'; you will soon recognise its influence in highlighting your professional potential and improving your prospects for promotion.

Name: ………………………………………..……..

Current Profession: ……………………………….

Professional role:…………………………………..

Describe the image & look you wish to create to help you promote yourself and provide opportunities for career advancements in the next:

6 mths …………………………………………….

TO:

Potential employers……………………………….

Customers………….………………………………

Fellow colleagues…………….....….….……………

2 years …………………………………………….

TO:

Potential employers……………………………….…..

Customers………….…………………………….……

Fellow colleagues…………….....….….…………….

The Golden rules for maintaining your Professional Image;

Colour; Keep to your personal colour scheme or coloured palette.

Clothing; consider & practice suggestions on; accessorising, home care and repair

Grooming; attention to the small details.

Chapter 12

Personal Image: Men's Interviews

Your image is your " Visual C.V" the silent yet vital 'visual communicator' of your professional status and potential it communicates your confidence and value of yourself, and is a major sales and marketing tool in gaining employment and promotion. The key areas to consider for an interview include: Image, Colour & Grooming.

Image

Your image should convey an understanding of the needs and demands expected of the job you are being interviewed for, with an image that reflects confidence and reliability in the qualities outlined in your C.V. and application. Your clothes should be appropriate for the industry sector being interviewed

Clothing should be comfortable and easy fitting; wear a Suit, Shirt and Tie. Suit; Medium to dark in colour, grey or blue suiting.

Pastel shirt; Plain or striped, long sleeved, classic collar; avoid patterned textiles which may distract the interviewer, avoid short sleeves.

Tie toned to suit and shirt colour, tied in a ½ Windsor knot, tail meeting waistband of trousers or longer avoid the "½ Mast look".

Shoes; comfortable and smart, polished and clean. Socks; solid knee length socks, colour toned to trousers and shoe colour, no visible skin.

Colour

Carefully consider your choice and combination of colours for your interview. Colours communicate a variety of messages;

Avoid grey towards your face it can create an unhealthy and ageing appearance.

Repeat your eye colour in accessories i.e. Ties, Frames of glasses this will encourage eye contact by highlighting your eyes and encourage the interviewer to focus on your face and on what you are saying.

Grooming

Grooming is one of your important and essential self marketing tools, it conveys your attention to detail, professionalism and self worth, consider the following;

- Have your hair restyled if you have had the same style for over a year. Hair should be washed, brushed, tidy, clean haircut. Tie long hair back from your face; avoid extreme haircuts, very short haircuts which may appear aggressive

- Teeth; clean fresh breath avoid spicy food, mouthwash, mints, no chewing gum.
- Deodorant; keep aftershave to minimum.
- Facial hair: neatly shaven, beards or moustaches trimmed and tidy. Nails; clean filed.
- Clothes; clean, ironed, stain & dust free, free of loose threads, buttons or stressed seams, pockets empty.
- Shoes; cleaned, polished, repaired.
- Accessories should be minimal and classic; rings to single pairs. Preferably wear a metal or leather strapped watch, metal pen rather than a disposable, a cotton handkerchief rather than a paper tissue.
- At your interview leave overcoats and unnecessary belongings in the reception area i.e. umbrella, bags to avoid appearing cluttered & disorganised on meeting your interviewer.

In a society which has become increasingly liberal in its ideas and expressions of personal identity there are still a few taboos which must be avoided for interviews. It is important to remember that your interviewer's view of what is acceptable or respectable can vary dramatically taboo areas to avoid:

- Garments with large slogans & brands.
- Fabrics: No transparent, leather, suede, floral or evening fabrics, highly patterned prints.
- Accessories; No Sport shoes or sandal, plastic carrier bags.
- Conceal; Body art or Tattoos where possible i.e. wear long shirt.

Exceptions to this are companies with a culture alien to dress codes and formality and are environments of self expression and creativity. It is necessary to fully understand the culture of the organisation you are being interviewed by. The only fundamental rule without exception is that no matter the culture of an organisation the following is still necessary to demonstrate order, discipline and respect for your prospective employer:

Grooming; clean, pressed and tidy clothing.

Hygiene; High level of personal hygiene and grooming.

Personal Image: Women's Interviews

Your image is your " Visual C.V" the silent yet vital 'visual communicator' of your professional status and potential it communicates your confidence and value of yourself, and is a major sales and marketing tool in gaining employment and promotion. The key areas to consider for an interview include: Image, Colour & Grooming.

Image

Your image should convey an understanding of the needs and demands expected of the job you are being interviewed for, with an image that reflects confidence and reliability in the qualities outlined in your C.V. and application. Your clothes should be appropriate for the industry sector being interviewed .

Clothing should be comfortable and easy fitting, wear a Skirt Suit/ Jacket or Blazer, Blouse, Accessories; Scarf & Jewellery. Conservative skirt length. Suit; Medium to dark, grey or blue, pastel/bright blouse. Plain, patterned or striped, long sleeved, classic high collar or neckline; avoid short sleeved blouses, and patterned textiles which may distract the interviewer.

Shoes; preferably heeled, slight heel, comfortable and smart, polished and clean.

Tights; always wear tights, solid colour toned to skirt and shoe colour, avoid seams or patterns. Always carry an extra pair of tights for an emergency.

Colour

Carefully consider your choice and combination of colours for your interview. Colours communicate a variety of messages;
Avoid grey towards your face it can create an unhealthy and ageing appearance. Repeat your eye colour in accessories i.e. Scarves/Ties, Earrings Frames of glasses this will encourage eye contact by highlighting your eyes and encourage the interviewer to focus on your face and on what you are saying.

Grooming

Grooming is one of your important and essential self marketing tools, it conveys your attention to detail, professionalism and self worth, consider the following;

- Have your hair restyled if you have had the same style for over a year. Hair should be washed, brushed, tidy, clean haircut. Tie long hair back from your face, avoid extreme haircuts.
- Teeth; clean fresh breath avoid spicy food, mouthwash, mints, no chewing gum.
- Deodorant; keep perfume to minimum.
- Remove or bleach facial hair. Nails; clean filed, light nail polish, no chipped nail polish.
- Makeup; subtle, fresh and light, not over done.
- Clothes; clean, ironed, stain & dust free, free of loose threads, buttons or stressed seams, pockets empty.
- Underwear: neutral i.e. white bra with white blouse, black bra with dark blouse.
- Shoes; cleaned, polished, repaired.
- Accessories minimal & classic; rings & earrings to single pairs, avoid dangling earrings & pendants, too many bangles. Preferably wear a metal or leather strapped watch, metal pen rather than a disposable pen, a cotton handkerchief rather than a paper tissue.
- At your interview leave overcoats and unnecessary belongings in the reception area i.e. umbrella, bags to avoid appearing cluttered & disorganised on meeting your interviewer.

In a society which has become increasingly liberal in its ideas and expressions of personal identity there are still a few taboos which must be avoided for interviews. It is important to remember that your interviewer's view of what is acceptable or respectable can vary dramatically taboo areas to avoid:

- Garments with large slogans & brands.
- Must wear supporting, under garments; i.e. no black bras under white blouses.
- Fabrics: No transparent, leather, suede, floral or evening fabrics, highly patterned prints.
- Accessories; No Sport shoes or sandal, plastic carrier bags.
- Conceal; Body art or Tattoos where possible i.e. wear long shirt or blouse.

Exceptions to this are companies with a culture alien to dress codes and formality and are environments of self expression and creativity. It is necessary to fully understand the culture of the organisation you are being interviewed by.

The only fundamental rule without exception is that no matter the culture of an organisation the following is still necessary to demonstrate order, discipline and respect for your prospective employer:

Grooming; clean, pressed and tidy clothing.

Hygiene; High level of personal hygiene and grooming.

Chapter 13

Personal Image : Presentations

Women's Preparation

- Wear a suit

- Blouse/ Shirt: Plain or minimal small pattern, long sleeves, classic high collar or neckline.

- Shoes; preferably heeled, slight heel, comfortable and smart, polished and clean.

- Makeup; conservative; try and wear at least some makeup.

- Nails should be manicured and clean avoid bright nail polish if liable to chip easily, otherwise go for a natural nail colour.

- Accessories should be minimal and classic; avoid excessive jewellery can be distracting, dangling earrings and pendants can be distracting, too many bangles, fad items, plastic carrier bags.

Men's Preparation

- Wear a Suit, Shirt & Tie.

- Plain or striped, long sleeved shirt, classic collar avoid. Avoid short sleeved shirts.

- Wear a ½ Windsor knot.

- Shoes; preferably laced.
- A cotton handkerchief not a paper tissue.
- If you must wear glasses aim for non reflective lenses

Colour

Avoid grey towards your face can create an unhealthy and ageing appearance. Repeat your eye colour in accessories i.e. Scarves, Earrings, frames of glasses; this will encourage eye contact by highlighting your eyes & encourage the audience to focus on your face & on what you are saying.

Carefully consider any use of excessive colour and patterns in garment; this may create a dancing effect with audience.

Socks; always wear solid colour socks toned to trousers and shoe colour. Tights; always wear tights, solid colour toned to skirt and shoe colour, avoid seams or patterns. Always carry an extra pair of tights in an emergency.

Grooming

Have your hair restyled if you have had the same style for over a year. Tie long hair back from your face as neatly as possible, clean and well groomed.

- Avoid extreme haircuts very short haircuts which may appear aggressive and threatening & anti-establishment.
- Clean teeth, manicured and clean nails, fresh breath and deodorant, minimal Perfume or Cologne if any.
- Add some translucent powder to your face to avoid high perspiration or cheek colouring & shining.
- For receding hairlines add a touch of translucent powder to pate to prevent shining.
- Lightly spray any fine unmanageable hair with hairspray.
- Clothing should be comfortable and easy fitting, clean, free of dust, wrinkles, loose threads & buttons, or stressed seams.
- Avoid anything too short or too tight.
- Empty your pockets, button up your jacket, otherwise audience will focus on your midriff.
- Double check all fastenings i.e. zips, buttons, linings, hemlines. Check collars are lying flat.
- If you must remove your jacket; enter with your jacket on and remove it at the beginning or during a natural break in the presentation and ask audiences permission; to maintain your professional stance and authority.

- Carefully consider any pattern on garments, may create a dancing effect with audiences eyes.
- If you must remove your jacket; enter with your jacket on and remove it at the beginning or during a natural break in the presentation and ask audiences permission; to maintain your professional stance and authority.
- Aim to create and convey an image of confidence by having an image of impeccable order.

Informal

Aim to appear approachable; with light to medium colours, express a personalised image.

Formal

Project a confident look, wear medium to dark suiting, pastel or bright shirt & an accent accessory in a bright colour.

Large Audiences

Create a theatrical impact with a strong visual image; grasp your audience's attention.

Choose striking colours, contrasting combinations or bold bright accent colours. Pay impeccable attention to detail from the fit of your outfit to your choice of accessories and personal grooming.

TV Presentations

Wear a well fitted suited with clear contours to the figure, particularly your shoulder and neckline.

Chapter 14

Care & Repair

It is important to recognise that with the proper aftercare you can ensure that your uniform retains its appearance and performs, giving maximum value for you and your staff.

Storing Garments

1. If possible always allow 24 hours in between wearing a garment again to extend its life and appearance for e.g. blouse or shirt 1 to wear, 1 in wash and (1 waiting.)
2. Always ensure garments are thoroughly dry and allow them to air before storing.
3. To retain garment appearance hang with zips & buttons fastened & pocket contents empty.
4. Store garments with room to hang freely without creasing.
5. Hang clothes on good quality hangers; avoid wire hangers.
   Waist supported hangers for skirts
   Trousers supported from hem, hung upside down or over padded trouser hanger.
6. Knitwear, soft and fine fabrics are best stored flat.

7. Brush garments regularly with a firm clothes brush.

8. Regularly check garments for stains or repairs i.e. loose buttons or hem lines and attend to a.s.a.p.

9. Creased garments; hang in bathroom and allow steam to release creases or alternatively place items which may be tumble dried, in drier with a damp towel for 5-10min.

10. Remove fluff from garments with double sided tape.

11. Remove all spare buttons and store in repair kit.

12. Carefully remove teaselling or bobbled pile from knitwear with disposable razor.

Cleaning Instructions

1. Wash garments frequently; but always follow individual care instructions on label.

2. Wash shirts and blouses after each wearing.

3. Wash heavily soiled garments separately.

4. Wash dark / bright garments before wearing and always wash; whites, darks and brights separately.

5. Dissolve washing powder completely before soaking garments.

Tumble drying

1. Synthetics may be warm tumble dried and pressed when slightly damp.

2. Cottons tumble dry and pressed when slightly damp.

Dry Cleaning

1. Check the label if the garment could or should be dry cleaned.

2. Dry clean garments with difficult or large stains.

Ironing

1. Check iron setting for each specific garment.

2. Order of ironing; Iron all seams, double and thick parts on the wrong side. Embroidered or applied badges should be pressed on the wrong side pressing onto a pad or with a cloth covering area & pressed on right side.

3. Iron small areas; collars, cuffs, then main body of garment.

4. Iron until all moisture is gone otherwise the article will crease when finally dry & air before storing.

Stain Removal

Any stain removal must be approached with care and common sense when possible request the advice of a professional i.e. Dry cleaner first.

Initial Treatment

- Always act immediately to any stains or accidents, initially blot with kitchen paper or an old white towel, solid stains should be lifted off the surface using a blunt knife or the bowl of a spoon.

- After checking cleaning instructions ensure you have the correct stain remover for the stain.

- Never use coloured rags or paper napkins on stains, chemicals can cause their colour to run.

- Initially don't over wet, use stain remover sparingly. To avoid ring marks; place the stained area over an absorbent cloth i.e. towel, work from the outside towards the centre to prevent it spreading, dabbing rather than rubbing.

- Always test stain removers on concealed inside seams; any problems consult dry cleaners.

- Begin with the simplest methods; soak in water and detergent followed by washing.

- Do not mix stain removal chemicals or bleach; may cause a chemical reaction or toxic gases.

- If you are unconfident seek the advice of a dry cleaner and inform them of what the stain is.

Stain	Solution
Collar & Cuff Dirt	Use biological liquid detergent as a pre-wash treatment by applying it gently with an old toothbrush. Then wash as usual.
Alcohol or food	Use soda water. Place towel under area. Fizz soda and rub in towards the centre spot.
Butter	Sponge with dry cleaning Fluid.
Chewing Gum	Scrape off; or you can freeze and harden the chewing gum by rubbing it with an ice cube placed in a plastic bag & sponge with dry cleaning fluid (before washing).
Chocolate	Sponge with mild soapy water.
Coffee & Tea	Sponge with glycerine or use warm water.
Egg	Scrape and sponge with soapy water.
Blood	Blot with concentrated common starch paste and rinse from the back with mild soapy water.
Lipstick	Rub white bread over the area firm but gentle or alternatively try a spot of vanish.
Glue	Sponge with methylated spirits.
Ink or Wine	Immerse in cold water./ Ink try dapping with cheap aftershave on cotton wool.
Grease, Tar, Car Oil	Sponge with dry cleaning fluid; immediate action for grease sprinkle with a tiny amount of talcum powder.
Iodine	Treat with cool water and then methylated spirits.
Iron Mould Rust marks	Sponge with lemon juice and cover with a thin layer of fine salt. Leave for an hour, rinse in cold water and launder as usual. Or Sponge with weak solution of oxalic acid until stain disappears then sponge carefully with household ammonia and rinse with water.
Mud	Once dry, brush and then sponge from the back with soapy water.
Tar	Put an absorbent white pad on top of the mark and apply eucalyptus oil on a cotton wool pad from below. Wash.
Candle wax	Scrape off surface wax. Place brown paper or paper towel over the stain and press with a warm iron. Spot with methylated spirit to remove any colour before washing.
Colour Run	Re wash in hottest water safe for fabric. You may need to soak whites in a colour run remover such as stain devils Colour Run Remover or Dylon Run Away.
Minor spots & stains	Use liquid detergent as a pre wash treatment by applying it neat with a toothbrush. Alternatively try a wet wipe.

Stain Removal

Care Symbols

Many of us are confused and unsure about the different Care label symbols. Below is a list of various symbols you may find during the process of caring for your uniform or personal wardrobe. Always read the individual care labels on garments in the context of the garments colour, fabric and decoration paying particular attention to guidance given on garments; embroidered or decorated with transfers, bead work etc.

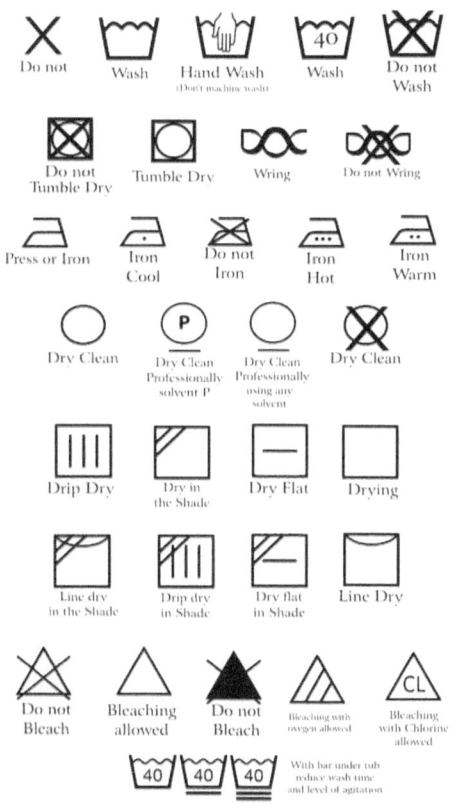

Chapter 15

Conclusion

Unfortunately since I have left the "Uniform industry" there is still no viable surveys or research to substantiate both the current customer's perception and underlining responses to image in the 21st Century. Offering little support for the employee, professional or business owner as to what the customer really subconsciously thinks with relation to "image" and the cultural shifts of the 21st Century.

Since I first wrote this book several years ago there has been a dramatic shift particularly in the UK in terms of visible self expression of one's Image in even the most traditional workplace environments. The display of tattoos, piercing to vibrant hair colours is commonplace and almost the norm in the workplace.

As an employee, business owner or professional we are left to answer the question ourselves whether as a culture we "Embrace a culture of Self expression" or are we still "A Culture which makes subconscious judgements rightly or wrongly" returning to my original example in Chapter 1 with George standing on Bond Street.

" Many stories can be told by our appearance, clothing, grooming, posture, facial expressions; it communicates our personality, attitude, emotions, economical and social status, sophistication and success."

Has the prospective customer or employers opinions really changed?

I will leave you on a personal note. Over the years my greatest challenge has been challenging my own self confidence and self image issues, sometimes our greatest weakness can become our greatest strength and obstacle to overcome in life. On graduating from Art College and setting up my first business it took my Aunt who I am very fond of and who loves me dearly to use a little tough love to tell me "You have to stop looking like an Art student and start looking like a professional if you are going to swap the creative world for the business world."

"Unfortunately not everyone has someone willing to say it as it is and tell you the uncomfortable truth".

I have been extremely fortunate through out my career to see the benefits that the right image can create, propelling someone's individual career or business to an entirely different level of achievement in both a creative and business environment.

I believe that you can use clothing as an essential business tool to create your own individual or teams "suit of armour".

I hope that my motivation to inspire others confidence and self esteem through clothing may help you in your career and business and reap the profits you deserve.

Goof luck in deciding what is honest and true for your organisation whether your company culture reflects and needs a corporate uniform or a culture of creative self expression.

Summary

Principle One; Image matters.

Principle Two; Be honest with your customer, what is your company really about.

Principle Three; Your staff's image must serve the needs of both your customer & your employee.

Principle Four; The visual representation of your business starts with your company brand, it is the template for every other visual element of your business.

Principle Five: The essential ingredients to a successful brand are; name, visibility, colour, styling.

Principle Six; Colour is the one essential visual tool in "Dressing for Business"

Principle Seven; What do we all remember? "Colour".

Principle Eight; Uniforms and Dress codes are not suitable for all organisations.

Principle Nine; Only implement a Company Uniforms if you have the resources to sustain, maintain a quality uniform that improves your staffs confidence & credibility.

Principle Ten; Ensure that your uniform supplier will provide a professional service that protects individual staff confidentiality.

Principle Eleven; Never agree to a uniform that devalues your professional image or credibility.

Bibliography & Reference Material

Sampson, Eleri. (1996) The Image Factor, Kogan Page, London.

Molly, John T. (1975) Dress for Success, Peter H Wyden, New York.

Molly, John T. New Dress For Success'. Image consultant to over 300 of Americas Fortune 500 Companies.

Reed Employment summary report; 11 April 1996. Sample of 641 organisations. Euro contracts 1996.

Further Information; Katy Nicholson or Sarah Parsons; Press Office Reed Personnel Services, 104 New Bond Street, London.

Discover more D.F. McKeever business books.

Are you an aspiring Entrepreneur?

Sign-up and receive your FREE Business Start-up Handbook <u>NOW!</u>

Learn about the 'The Designovation ® Philosophy'

"*30 years research of Great Entrepreneurs & their Enterprises*"

Available in both E-book & paperback

Part One The Entrepreneur; White Ball Thinking

Part Two The Enterprise; Black Box Thinking

Please visit us Now!

http://www.designovation.co.uk/about

Customer Comments

Over 18 years as Business wear supplier we provided various training programmes and workshops on personal & professional image designed for students, graduates, corporate groups, professionals and women returnees to work.

'I'll never look at my wardrobe in the same way again!' Keith.

'Never thought it was going to be very relevant or interesting to begin with - but was soon proven wrong.' David.

'Thought provoking, lots of advice gave me a lot to think about my Personal Image'. June.

'Presentation was very thorough and useful. In particular, involvement with the audience, e.g. choosing a member of the audience and discussing eye colour, clothing etc., Very informative.' Alistair.

'Good to hear a new point of view on a subject that is usually not considered in the Business Community.' Rhona.

'Very informative and very well thought out. You've pointed out things I may never have thought about with regards to Image.' Louise.

'Your appearance in general backs up your presentation very well and has prompted me to consider my appearance more carefully'. Andy.

'Good involvement with us and introduced us into presentation which helped for personal decisions. Comparatives and differences shown by slides were very helpful and gave the point, Excellent.' Lynn.

'Food for thought......and smashed a few pre-conceived ideas.' Jamie.

'It was such a worthwhile topic we have asked Burns Dezign to present on further 10 programmes and will continue.' Training Manager.

About the Author

D.F. McKeever is a Scottish Author & Illustrator. She lives in Scotland with her husband and three children. Her passion and interest in both self help & business began in her early teens while working in the family business. After graduating with a B.A. Honours in Design she went on to build her own retail & design business, which she operated for 18 years servicing the public & private sector in Scotland with the supply of Corporate Uniforms.

www.ingramcontent.com/pod-product-compliance
Lightning Source LLC
Chambersburg PA
CBHW021422210526
45463CB00001B/489